One day in
Russia 1917

DAY BOOK SERIES

Acknowledgements

We should like to express our gratitude to all those who have kindly granted copyright permission for photographs in this volume, and special thanks to our illustrators.

Imperial War Museum: pages 9 (top), 11 (top), 12, 15 (bottom), 16 (top), 27 (top), 30, 35 (top)

Mansell Collection: pages 4, 9 (bottom), 10 (bottom), 11 (bottom), 15 (top), 16 (bottom), 23 (bottom), 25 (top), 27 (bottom), 34 (top), 35 (bottom), 36 (top), 38, 39, (top), 42

Novosti Press Agency: pages 10 (top), 17 (top), 18 (top), 31 (bottom), 32, 33, 34 (bottom), 37, 39 (bottom), 41

Nicholas Turner: pages 24 (top), 29 (top)

Eric Kincaid: illustrations, pages 5, 18 (bottom)

Cecilia Ware: line drawings and illustration, pages 8 (top), 17 (bottom), 20, 40

Rosemary Holliday: illustration, page 7

All other pictures are from the Tyndall Photographic Library

First United States Publication, 1975

Copyright © 1974 by Robert Tyndall Ltd.

ISBN: 0-200-00146-9

Library of Congress Catalog Card Number: 74-25541

Printed in Great Britain

1 2 3 4 5 6 7 8 9 10

One day in Russia 1917

by Philip Bolsover

Abelard-Schuman
New York

Above: Map showing Russia and surrounding states, some of which became independent immediately after the Bolshevik Revolution in November 1917

Opposite, left to right: Madame Etienne Lafarge, Boris Melnikov, Tamara Ivanova, Major Vasili Sokolov, Nikolai Saratov, Mikhail Yanishev

Contents

AD 1917

Introduction

History is fun; but a list of unconnected accounts of battles and events is not.

History is the story of how we, the human race, lived, governed, fought and learned in years gone by. The influence of one people upon another, and often of one man upon a nation, is crucial to the development of civilization.

In this series, we look at the customs and events of an age, and history is shown through the eyes of those who were living at the time.

Each book in this series is intended as an introduction to a period, and great care has been taken to see that all illustrations, photographs and artwork are accurate. Where an illustration is not specifically from the year in which the book is set, the caption explains its relevance and, wherever possible, its date.

Words in italics in the text (italicized only at their first appearance) are explained in the Glossary, and there is further information on some aspects of the times in the General Notes. An Index is provided for easy reference, but it is recommended that the book be read as a whole to begin with.

Having had a taste of the atmosphere of the age, you may be interested to read more about some of the people, their homes, politics, literature, society, religious beliefs and customs. There is a Further Reading list at the back of the book, but this represents only a small number of the many books available. Have a look in your library and see what you can find.

MORNING

In a deserted mansion, not very far from the center of St. Petersburg – *Petrograd*, as it was now called – November's gray dawn revealed two boys and a girl sleeping comfortably on the ornate gilt couches of a neglected, but still impressive, salon. They might have been three bundles of rags, curiously out of place in all this fading luxury of polished floors, thick velvet curtains, long mirrors and shining walnut tables.

Seven months had elapsed since the owner of the mansion, Prince Oblomov, dismayed by the overthrow of the *Romanov Tsars* after 300 years of imperial power, had, with other aristocratic families, hurriedly left the country. Already over this dust-covered splendor there was an air of creeping decay, reinforced now by the dawn mist that stole in stray wisps through a broken pane in one of the big windows.

To 12-year-old Boris Melnikov, though, opening his eyes and sitting up, all at once wide awake and wary, this was unimaginable magnificence. He had never seen anything like it. When he and his companions had broken in through

Drawing showing a Balaclava helmet of the type worn by Russian soldiers on active service

Sketch showing the defeat and flight of the Tsar's army in the Ukraine

the window at dusk, the room was half lost in shadow; but now, in the strengthening light, it was a revelation.

Boris shook the other two awake, and together they prowled curiously around the great room. They had come together by chance in the streets during the previous night – Shura, a year older than Boris, Anna, 12 but looking older, and Boris. They all wore dirty gray blouses, belted at the waist with string. Boris was lucky; somewhere he had found a pair of *valinki*, high felt boots that would keep his feet and legs warm in the rapidly approaching winter. The valinki were stuffed with paper and bits of rag. Shura and Anna had sacking wound closely around their legs above broken boots. Anna, like the others, wore baggy trousers that disappeared into the sacking and, over her shoulders, down to the waist, a piece of *khaki* canvas with a hole cut in it for her head. Her hair was tucked into a woollen *Balaclava* helmet, obviously once army property – as were the peaked khaki caps worn by the boys. All in all, their clothing was peculiar but warm and fairly rainproof. They looked not very different from hundreds of other children now roaming the streets, victims of war and the chaos of past months. They scratched themselves automatically as they explored the room, and their smell was very different from the perfumes that had once pervaded this air.

"But where's the grub?" said Boris suddenly. Six months of street life had taught him to think of essentials. Three years ago, his father had become one of the fifteen million men in the Tsar's army, conscripted to fight the Germans. That was the last Boris saw of him. Two years later, he was dead, one of the four million killed and wounded in the dreadful rout of the biggest army the world had ever seen. Never before had any nation suffered such horrible losses in so short a time.

After that, life was hard for Boris and his mother, as it was for thousands of other widows and their families when food became scarce and prices soared. One day his mother came home with a man he had never seen before. On the following day, Boris was given a *rouble* and sent out to stand in one of the long lines for bread – where people waited for hours, sometimes all night. When Boris came home, his mother and her friend had gone.

That was when street life began for Boris. Now, he was independent, sharp, cheeky and cheerfully ruthless – he had to be, as it was not easy to scratch a living from the streets, and there was a lot of competition. Shura and Anna, for instance, were friendly enough and company for a night, but their experiences were similar to his and they, too, had to make a living – bread did not grow on trees.

"Yes," they said, "Grub – where is it?" But there was none. They found the kitchens, but there was nothing eatable there – only bread long since moldy, flour that was full of weevils, rotten potatoes, cakes that had turned green – and everywhere signs of rats and mice. It was all rather horrible, this musty rottenness in the midst of luxury.

"Let's go," said Anna, "We've got to eat; we'll starve here."

So they took tea from a box, found some matches (those were precious), cut strips of velvet from the curtains to wrap around their feet and legs – it was softer than sacking – and left that dying house. In fact, it didn't die; a year later it was a school, loud with laughter and shouting and quarreling, as full of life as it had ever been – just a different life. Boris, Anna and Shura could not know this as they climbed through the window into streets where world-shaking things were happening.

Soon after the three youngsters made their way into the street, Madame Lafarge, wife of a member of the French Embassy staff, sat up in bed for her morning coffee. She had been awakened early by the sound of distant rifle shots. This was becoming altogether too familiar, she reflected as she sipped the coffee and thought back to that earlier revolution of the previous *March*.

With the defeats and hardships of the *war*, resentment had simmered into desperation and finally boiled over into action. There had been the great strikes and demonstrations led by 30,000 workers from the now famous *Putilov* metal plant; the peasant revolt against the landowners; the mass desertions from the army; and, simultaneously, the creation of *soviets*, or councils of workers in factories, peasants in villages, soldiers and sailors in the armed forces.

The Tsar's government, aware of growing discontent,

Above: A soldier searches a civilian for firearms on the streets of Petrograd. **Below:** Portrait of Nicholas II, last Emperor and Tsar of Russia

Above: A party of Cossacks on patrol. Note their distinctive headgear. **Below:** Peter the Great (1672–1725), Emperor of Russia. In 1703 he created St. Petersburg as the new capital

had prepared an elaborate military plan to deal with revolt, and had brought in 160,000 soldiers to strengthen the city's garrison. But in the end this was worse than useless, for the soldiers, many of them newly conscripted from factories and villages, joined the demonstrators, taking their arms with them. For a while the *Cossacks*, armed with lances and rifles, fierce and picturesque on their shaggy little horses each with a truss of hay tied to its saddle, charged the crowds; but they held their fire and used only the flat of their *sabers*, so that in the end people realized that their charges were mere show. Crowds even cheered them when it was obvious that the Cossacks were protecting people from the hated police.

Madame Lafarge reflected sadly that even the Guards and the *Preobrazhensky* regiment, founded generations ago by *Peter the Great* as a royal bodyguard, formed soviets and refused to leave their barracks. That was a bitter blow, particularly as the officers – all from the nobility – were humiliated and badly treated by their men. Madame Lafarge recalled that Count Louis de Robien, a diplomat in the French Embassy, had talked to her about a young friend, an officer in a Guards regiment, whose career was now in ruins. "Indeed," said the count, "it can be no joke being an officer at the moment, considering that in this regiment they are obliged to have their meals in the barracks with their men."

Street barricades appeared, guarded by men who had mysteriously acquired arms. Trucks and armored cars, confiscated by mutinous soldiers, roved the streets. "Down with the Tsar!" the banners had said. "Send the German woman home!" The *Tsarina Alexandra* was German by birth, though she had been brought up by her grandmother, *Queen Victoria*, in Britain.

Listening to the gunfire on the morning of November 7, Madame Lafarge recalled that the earlier revolution had flared into action on March 8. The date stuck in her memory because on that same day the Tsar had gone to the front to take charge of his armies, leaving the Tsarina to conduct affairs at home.

"My brain is resting here," wrote *Nicholas II*, who was in many ways a mild, well-meaning man, though he had

always declared stubbornly that he would rule as an *autocrat*. "Here there are no ministers, no troublesome questions demanding thought." Then, apparently unable to comprehend the dangers surrounding him and the misery of his people, he added a sentence that was either stupid or callous, according to one's viewpoint, considering the hardships of life under his regime: "I shall take up dominoes in my spare time!"

He soon had plenty of time for dominoes. On March 15, he was told by the generals of his armies and the leading members of the *Duma* that he must abdicate. He proposed to pass the crown to his brother, *Grand Duke Michael*, but the soldiers and the Petrograd Soviet would have none of it: "Horse-radish is no sweeter than radish," was their reply. A week later Nicholas II was a prisoner in his own palace at *Tsarskoe Selo*, near Petrograd. The Tsarina was busy with her children, who had measles.

Above: Supporters of the Revolution removed the Tsar's portrait from the Duma and destroyed other relics of the old regime. **Below:** Grand Duke Michael, in the foreground, with his personal staff

Madame Lafarge had heard the demonstrators from the factories and the soldiers singing the *Marseillaise* in the streets – it was a favorite revolutionary song – but she admitted that even the French Revolution could not compare with this. Only 46 years ago, 80 per cent of Russians were *serfs*, the property of landlords, like cattle or dogs. Three years ago, when the war broke out in 1914, the Russian monarchy, ruling ruthlessly over 148 million people, was menaced by revolt, but was still the most powerful on earth, feared by half of Europe. Now that the Romanovs had gone, the *Republic* was here – and by the look of things it would soon be the world's first *socialist* republic. What an incredible change from the luxury and excesses of the court life under the Tsars.

Madame Lafarge was still thinking about those March days as she dressed. Sometimes the soldiers and the demon-

The police had confiscated the people's flour. During the Revolution the police stations were raided and large quantities of the flour were taken to the Duma which then distributed it among the poor

strators had been polite, even kind; sometimes they were wild and brutal – particularly with the hated police, whose stations they sacked and burned. She remembered passing one police station with the Countess de Robien, when a grand piano came hurtling from a window to land on the pavement with a crash, its strings vibrating.

Some houses of the nobility were burned and their owners arrested. General Stackelberg, partly French, was killed in front of his wife and his body thrown into the *River Neva*. Officers had to appear before the Soviet committee composed of students and private soldiers. They were roughly pushed to a table after having their badges of rank stripped from them, and were handed identity certificates. Often they were set to the hardest and most humiliating work, particularly in the navy.

Madame Lafarge remembered another incident. A group of demonstrators, mostly women, were marching along singing menacing songs to hymn tunes. "We'll loot, we'll burn, we'll cut their throats," they sang – yet as they passed a chapel they religiously crossed themselves. At another time, the Grand Duke Michael, angry because the French diplomats had been instructed not to go to his house, shouted icily to the French Ambassador, "Use the back stairs, if you're afraid."

That was funny in its way. It was not funny, however, to visit Countess Kleinmichel and find that the guards in her house had stolen things, ruined tapestries and used her big drawing room as a meeting place for the area soviet. The room was full of wooden trestle tables, the floor filthy, the carpets gone. . . .

"Ah," sighed Madame Lafarge sadly to herself, as she stepped into the street – the shooting had stopped – "Ah, what will happen to our lovely Russia, what will happen to us all . . . what will happen to me?"

It was cold on the roof of the railway carriage. Mikhail Yanishev, private soldier in the 408th *Kuznetsk* Infantry Regiment, wore a long army greatcoat that hung down to his ankles; somehow, he had managed to acquire a civilian fur hat that came down to his eyebrows, with flaps over his ears. Inside high leather boots, his legs and feet were

Russian soldiers on the march

wrapped in rags, but still he was cold as he crouched down, hands tucked into his sleeves, while the overloaded train rumbled along slowly. The carriages were packed with soldiers and civilians; men covered the roofs and hung on to the sides of the coaches, like grapes on a vine.

It was a miserable journey in the raw, freezing November weather, but to Mikhail and the rest of the soldiers only one thing mattered – they were going away from the front, they were going home. Mikhail was one in a million – or a million and a half, no one knew the exact figure – who had made this journey home, on foot or by whatever transportation they could find. The biggest army in the world was dissolving to create the biggest mutiny in the world.

For generations, the Tsar's army had been notorious for the brutality of its officers and the submission of its men. The whip and the fist were instruments of discipline. A man could be flogged for failing to carry out an order, beaten for a mistake at drill or for not saluting smartly enough, punched in the face at any time by a drunken officer. "A soldier's face is like a tambourine: the harder you hit it the happier you feel," the men joked bitterly.

That was bad enough, but when in the first year of the war food became meager, clothing inadequate, ammunition scarce, when every battle was lost and men died by the hundreds of thousands, why then it was time even for the Russian soldier to say "enough." A man in Mikhail's regiment wrote home: "We stand in the trenches. Cold, mud and vermin. Food once a day at 10 o'clock at night, and that lentils so black that a pig wouldn't eat it. We're starving to death. . . ." And later: "Our regiment refused to advance. Some went, but others wouldn't leave the trenches, so I didn't crawl out."

Meanwhile, war *profiteers* were making millions of roubles from army contracts for supplies, clothing and *shells* that never reached the front. Mikhail and every soldier knew this.

Officers, desperately trying to maintain discipline, became harsher than ever. But now the soldiers retaliated, and it was the officers' turn to suffer. The soldiers had a song which emphasized their mutinous spirit:

Russian troops break their journey to the trenches, in the winter of 1915, to prepare a hot meal beside the train. Conditions for the soldiers returning in 1917 were a good deal less comfortable

Oh, orphan me,
To the woods I'll go,
The woods deep and black,
With my rifle on my back,
I'll go hunting.
Three deeds I'll do:
The first black deed,
My captain off I'll lead,
The second black deed,
Put my rifle to his head,
The third black deed,
Right there I'll shoot him dead.
Cursed son of a bitch,
My captain.

By the early part of 1917, soldiers and sailors were forming councils that took complete control of their regiments; officers could act only with their approval. The support of these councils for the March revolution brought the overthrow of the Tsar and the formation of a *Provisional Government* consisting mainly of "moderate" socialists, liberal intellectuals and the property-owning classes. This was not the government to end the war.

But the soldiers cried "Peace," and to this they added two other demands, put forward by the *Bolsheviks* under *Lenin*, "Bread and Land." From that moment, the slogan "Peace, Bread and Land" dominated every demonstration.

The two Provisional Governments, in which the most powerful figure was *Alexander Kerensky*, a clever politician and emotional orator, did not respond to any of these three demands. They failed to provide more food, they did not help the peasants, who were themselves taking the land – and above all, they declared that the war must go on, the army must fight.

At a meeting of the Petrograd Soviet on October 30, a soldier opened his speech with the bitter words, *"Comrades! I bring you greetings from the place where men are digging their graves and calling them trenches."* The whole army, he shouted, would support the demand for peace. In fact they were, as Lenin pointed out, voting for that demand "with their feet"; they were walking out of the war.

That was why Mikhail was riding on the roof of a

Above: A compelling portrait of Lenin preaching the spirit of Revolution. **Below:** A crowd gathered before the Duma. The banners bear the slogan "Land and Freedom"

Above: Soldiers traveling on the footboard of a motorcar with red flags fixed to their bayonets.
Below: Kerensky (top left) with members of the Provisional Government

railway carriage toward his village. He had two strong reasons for making this cold, desperate journey. First, he refused to be killed or wounded in a war he hated; and second, as a peasant, he wanted to be in his village when the land was shared out.

So here he was, with a multitude of others, spreading like a flood across the face of Russia from a battlefront fifteen hundred miles long – and Mikhail, like most of the others, had brought his gun with him.

Major Vasili Sokolov, marching down the *Nevsky Prospect* in Petrograd with a battalion of the Finland Reserve Regiment, allowed his thoughts to wander. Life was so difficult now. The war was hateful, but if the mutineers had their way Russia would be defeated and occupied, bound by intolerable terms.

The major, from a middle-class, liberal family, had welcomed the overthrow of the old *regime*. The March revolution had his cautious approval; the country had needed fresh ideas, new methods, a chance for good businessmen and technicians to spread their wings, an end to censorship, and more scope for the professions.

But, thought the major, eyeing with distaste a tattered group of civilian *Red Guards*, each with a red arm-band and a rifle, things had got out of hand. There was no discipline. Saluting had been abolished, rank had been abolished, generals obeyed committees of loutish private soldiers; officers in the Guards tore off their medals, burned their epaulettes and dared not raise their voices to a corporal. The army had been held together by the *knout*, the lash; that was bad, but now the lash had gone, the death penalty had been abolished, and what had followed seemed like chaos.

It was true that behind him the battalion was marching in fairly good order to a tune from the ballet of *The Little Hunch-backed Horse* – but they carried red flags and there were red rags on the men's bayonets. Also, had he not himself seen, only a few days ago, a group of eight old generals going to take an oath of allegiance before the Duma, each one of them wearing a red arm-band?

Red Guards firing from an armoured freight tram during the October 1917 battles in Moscow

An example of a Red Guard arm-band with the inscription "February 27th 1917 RED GUARD Vasilyevsky Island District"

27 февраля 1917 года

КРАСНАЯ ГВАРДІЯ

Васильевского Острова

Above: Painting of a meeting of the Petrograd Soviet of Workers' and Soldiers' Deputies, held on November 7, 1917. Lenin is addressing the meeting

Tamara Ivanova

It was not surprising though, for the Petrograd Garrison was now run by the new Soviet of Soldiers' and Workers' *Deputies*. The Soviet, back in March, had passed an order telling every unit in the armed forces to elect a committee of the lower ranks to run the affairs of the unit, and send a representative to the Soviet. Arms, said the order, were to be under the control of company and battalion committees and were not in any circumstances to be issued to officers. So the revolver holster at the major's side was empty.

Vasili Sokolov recalled his amazement when he read in the order: "Officers' titles such as Your Excellency, Your Honour, etc., are abolished and are replaced by such forms of address as Mr. General, Mr. Colonel, etc." So now after ten years in the army, he was "Mr. Major" – and very polite to his men. "Rudeness to soldiers by officers", said the order, "is forbidden, and all infractions of this rule must be reported by the soldier to his company committee."

"Please, Mr. Corporal . . .", muttered the major, derisively, to himself. "Please, Mr. Soldier, will you march in step?" How could you run an army like that? And with the Germans ready to march in!

That order was the famous Order No. 1, written at the dictation of a group of soldiers as a result of a resolution passed at the first meeting of the Soviet on March 1. Later, Kerensky said he would gladly have sacrificed ten years of his life "that the order might never have been signed". But Sobolev, Assistant Commissar of the Northern Front, reported to Kerensky in October, "Today we have almost no army; tomorrow we will have no army at all."

The end of *Tsarism*, thought the liberal Major Sokolov, was all very fine, a democratic revolution was all very well, but now discipline was needed, discipline everywhere. Faintly in the distance he heard the sound of rifle-fire; it hardly interrupted his troubled thoughts, for it was not unusual nowadays. . . . He could not know that the *second revolution* had started.

The bread line stretched down the street and was lost in darkness. Tamara Ivanova had been waiting since five o'clock that morning and it was now nearly eight o'clock. But some women had been there all night, so Tamara was a long way down the queue, and she was not at all sure that she would get any bread. Not that it was marvellous when you did get it – rough black stuff – but, still, it was food, and there was little enough of that.

The queue was nearly all women. In the darkness you could hardly tell one from the other. They were mostly short and thickset, like the majority of Russian women. They wore long felt boots, dark skirts down to their ankles, grey shawls and coats wrapped closely round them and scarves, white or coloured, over their hair and ears. They talked continuously and bitterly of their many problems: the cost of living, the profiteering, the difficulty of getting food, clothing or anything else – and, of course, the war, for every woman in the queue had some member of her family killed or wounded.

A contemporary Russian artist's view of a bread queue, a common sight in Petrograd

After an American cartoon of 1905. This shows that, years before the final Bolshevik insurrection of 1917, the Russian peasant was seen to be oppressed by forces, at that time beyond his control—Cossackism, incompetence, despotism, religious intolerance, graft, oppressive taxation, greed, exile and, worst of all, by bureaucracy in the shape of the Tsar with his robe and crown. The peasant holds a small axe which represents the National Assembly, the hope of parliamentary reformers

Tamara worked in a textile factory nearby. She would be late for work again, she told herself – but she would not be the only one, not by a long way. The factory committee would make allowances and the boss could do very little about it. She hoped her room would be safe while she was away. It was dark from three in the afternoon to ten in the morning now, and robberies were increasing, though the men with loaded rifles were taking turns at guard duty all night.

"Milk's up again," said Tamara to her neighbour in the line, "forty *kopeks* a *krushka* now – and it was seven kopeks before the war." Actually, you were lucky to get any at all; the papers said there was only enough for half the babies in the city. And as for bread, the ration dropped every week; it was down this week to a quarter of a pound a day.

"And tea," said her friend. "Eighteen roubles now – it used to be four-and-a-half." "But shoes," grumbled Tamara, "I can't get a pair for my man at less than 144 roubles, but I can remember buying a pair for 12 just before the war. It's worse if he tries to mend his old ones – 400 roubles for a piece of leather; imagine it!"

Wages had gone up, of course, but prices had increased more than twice as fast. So Tamara and her friends were angry as they talked together. They were tired of standing in queues, tired of paying enormous prices, tired of being without heating. In fact some of them had done more than grumble; they had taken food by force and wrecked shops.

The militant mood of the women was common knowledge. They had been the first to riot in the March days, and they were at the front of every demonstration. Nowadays, the soldiers were almost always friendly and ready to join the demonstrators, but if they were hostile, the women, Tamara among them, would go forward and grasp the bayonets with their bare hands, surround the soldiers and argue with them. Then the soldiers, individually or in groups, would slip from the ranks and disappear into the crowd. Entire battalions had disintegrated in this way.

Detail from a contemporary painting showing Lenin addressing a meeting of workers at the Putilov factory in Petrograd in 1917

Even before the March revolution the Government had been afraid of the women. In January, a secret police report to the Minister of the Interior (made public later) said: "Mothers of families, exhausted by endless waiting in the lines at the shops, and suffering at the sight of their half-starved and sick children, are perhaps nearer to revolution than Messrs. *Milyukov, Rodichev* & Co. [anti-Tsarist politicians] and are, of course, much more dangerous, because they represent a powder *magazine* which requires only a spark to explode."

An armoured car came rumbling down the street. On its sides were painted the slogans that now adorned half the public buildings in Petrograd, "Down with war!", "Land and Freedom!" A soldier with a red arm-band waved. Tamara's eyes followed the car with approval.

Nikolai Saratov, manager and part-owner of the textile factory in which Tamara worked, was seething with rage as he sat in his office reading the document sent to him by the factory council. It listed eight demands for improvements in pay and working conditions, but it was the sheer arrogance of Article Nine that infuriated Saratov: "Meanwhile," it said, "the owner shall not be allowed to sell or lease his factory – because it is soon to be ours."

"That", thought Saratov, grimly, "remained to be seen." The cool cheek of them! His father and his grandfather before him had owned this factory. They had worked all their lives to keep the place going, just as he had himself. If they had made a profit, well they had risked their capital, and they had given steady employment to a lot of people who had no idea of how to run a factory themselves.

So this was the answer to something that had been puzzling him for weeks. He had kept asking himself why the workers had become so tender with his property. They had suppressed the hotheads who wanted to wreck the place in the heat of the revolution; they had appointed a committee to guard against robbery; they kept telling each other to be careful with the machines. Now he knew why.

"Well, the factory committee had better look out," muttered Saratov. They would do well to remember that *Skobelev*, the Minister of Labour, had issued an order a

Satirical cartoon showing Skobelev, one of the Menshevik party, who became Minister of Labour in the Coalition Government

month ago forbidding works committees to meet during working hours or to interfere with the hiring and firing of workers. That would clip their wings if it was enforced. The trouble was that up to now nobody had taken any notice – the committees had gone on in their old ways and employers had been weak. Saratov sighed. He was really not in a position to criticize; after all, he was himself meeting the works council that very afternoon during working hours.

Impatiently, he threw the council's document aside. So many problems! He had done well out of army contracts since 1913, the year before the war began, and he could still do well. But he could not get the raw materials – or, at least, not a quarter of what he needed. What about the machines, too? They would not run for ever without spare parts or oil. The railways were chaotic, they just did not deliver; and electricity – the power stations seemed to switch the current off and on as the whim took them. It had been off this morning – perhaps some electricity worker had indigestion.

Saratov began to make notes for the meeting. He would tell them a thing or two this time. . . .

Above: During the "July Days" armed revolutionaries incited the Putilov workers to support the violent opposition to the Provisional Government. **Below:** The Revolutionaries disrupted main services and supplies in Petrograd, and are shown here outside the telephone office

AFTERNOON

Mikhail Yanishev was glad to drop off the train when it made one of its many unscheduled stops, only a mile or two from his village. He was happy to be talking with old friends in his father's cottage. The days when a deserter would have to hide in the woods had gone. But some of the men, and women, were still critical of anybody who left the front. They were suspicious, too, about what was happening in the cities, particularly in Petrograd and in *Moscow*.

His village was in fertile country and more prosperous than most, but it was no more than a collection of wooden shacks lighted in the mid-afternoon dusk by oil lamps and candles. The unpaved village street had turned to deep mud in the November sleet, but soon it would be frozen over and easy to use again. In summer the fields and woods were warm and peaceful, the river rich in fish. It was a quiet, beautiful place, and Mikhail loved it dearly.

Above: Many peasants were highly skilled craftsmen, in the service of the Tsar. This detail from a door, decorated in gold, in the Winter Palace shows the intricacy of their work. **Below:** An idealized picture of a collective farm (1935), one of the aspirations of the Revolution

"We heard about the revolution a week after it started," Mikhail's father was saying. "So we turned out the old police and chose a district council to send delegates to Petrograd. You know all the good land around here belonged to the Tsar, but we drove off the Tsar's officials and decided to farm his land ourselves. It was hard, though, because the army had taken all the men except the old and the sick. We worked all day and in June, when the nights were short, we worked nearly all night too. But by that time a lot of the boys were back – you're a late one."

This was too much for one of the old man's friends. "We sent grain and hay to the army," he said, "and some of us said we'd go there ourselves if the boys didn't fight. We've got to fight. If we don't those German generals will have the Tsar back in no time." This started a fierce argument that went on until Mikhail could stand it no longer.

"You don't know what it's like," he shouted. "We've been there nearly three years. The boys are tired. They'll not fight any more. And if they don't come back who will

Left: Contemporary sketch of miserable Russian soldiers writing home from the trenches. **Above:** Even civilians suffered considerable hardship during the severe winters. Here men are cutting ice to unblock the River Neva

help you when you can't work the fields any more? How many of you have lost a son, how many have a cripple in the family now? Go on, put your hands up!" About two-thirds lifted their hands. "Well, then. . . ." said Mikhail. And for the moment there was no more argument.

Later, Mikhail's father told him how there was now a network of village councils in the district. The representatives of 27 councils had met to elect three delegates to the All-Russian Soviet of Peasants that was to meet in Petrograd. "We don't care about parties," he said. "All we want is land and freedom. Whoever wants that is a revolutionist."

He admitted that some of the peasants and the deserters had burned manor houses and killed the landlords; and he was glad he had not been there.

Madame Lafarge was uneasy. Something dreadful was happening. She could feel it in the streets. She knew, of course, that an immense change had taken place in March and that events had been moving since July towards a new crisis. July had perhaps been the last chance, for that was when *General Kornilov* had almost managed to rescue poor Russia from its plight. He had massed a lot of loyal troops just when people, even some of the workers, were beginning to oppose Kerensky and his Provisional Government – they were tired of the food shortages, the demonstrations, the speeches and decrees, the strikes and the hooligans who threatened honest people or robbed their homes.

Kerensky had been in a dilemma. He had himself appointed General Kornilov commander-in-chief of the army, but then Kornilov had turned against him. Now Kornilov's troops were approaching Petrograd. He might even restore the monarchy and bring back the Tsar. In desperation, Kerensky had appealed to the Petrograd Soviet and the Bolsheviks, who were his harshest critics. Then, significantly, the army – or the greater part of it, including the 160,000 men of the Petrograd garrison – got ready to fight, not against the Germans but against Kornilov.

Factory workers were given rifles, barricades were built across the main streets, but the people who really defeated Kornilov were the railwaymen. The trainloads of Kornilov's

Workers behind their barricades in the streets of Petrograd

Above: People panic as a shot is fired in the Nevsky Prospect. **Below:** Alexander III of Russia

troops, dispatched to take Petrograd, were shunted into sidings or taken away from, instead of to, Petrograd. That was the end of Kornilov. His defeat made the Bolsheviks stronger than ever, and now, Madame Lafarge felt, they were making use of their strength.

This afternoon, she decided, as she walked home from a party at the British Embassy, through streets that were empty except for groups of Red Guards or army lorries carrying troops with fixed bayonets, things were different.

During the March revolution it was still possible to live almost unaware of the tremendous events that were taking place. True, the statue of *Catherine the Great* in front of the *Alexandrinsky Theatre* bore a little red flag in its hand, and there were similar decorations on all the public buildings; of course, the great bronze statue of *Alexander III* was pulled down and children had stood triumphantly on its prone head; certainly great demonstrations of soldiers, sailors and civilians sometimes blocked the streets. If you ignored the wartime shortages, though, and the dreadful poverty of many people, you could say that things looked fairly normal on, for instance, the Nevsky Prospect.

Crowds were shopping, tramcars were running, gambling clubs were open, restaurants were full of well-dressed people – young ladies who had come from the provinces to mix in society, and glittering young officers. It was true that when a middle-class lady went out to tea she often carried half a loaf of bread in her muff and a little silver box full of sugar, but, nevertheless, the parties went on, the theatres were full, the ballet was popular, the intelligentsia argued interminably about affairs totally unconnected with politics or the war.

"The daughter of a friend of mine came home one afternoon in hysterics because a woman street-car conductor called her – Comrade," wrote *John Reed*, a left-wing American journalist Madame Lafarge had met when the embassy gave a press conference.

It was he who reminded her that Peter the Great's *Tabel o Ravgov* still held good, and almost everybody, from schoolboy up, except peasants and workers, wore a prescribed uniform with the insignia of the Emperor on

Earlier in 1917, during the February uprisings, many generals were arrested by the Revolutionaries and thereafter their powers were severely limited

buttons and shoulder strap. One member of the Duma had gone to a meeting in civilian clothes, and had been turned away because he was not wearing the prescribed Tsar's uniform.

When Madame Lafarge went into an expensive café for a cup of coffee, there was a sign on the walls saying, "No tips! Just because a man has to make his living as a waiter there is no need to insult him by offering him a tip!"

In the café, Madame Lafarge talked to a wealthy Russian, Lianozov, known as the "Russian *Rockefeller*", a right-wing liberal in politics. "Revolution", he told her, "is a sickness. Sooner or later the foreign powers must intervene here, as one would intervene to cure a sick child and teach it how to walk." He wanted the Government to leave Petrograd for Moscow now that the Germans were at *Riga*. Then a state of siege could be declared and the loyal troops, aided by the Germans, could overthrow the Bolsheviks.

Lianozov and Madame Lafarge talked of their many friends in the aristocracy who were suffering under the new regime. The great houses were being occupied by soldiers or *bureaucrats*, or else they had been sold and the money smuggled out of the country. The banks had got

Above: One of the palaces built by Peter the Great, as it appears today. **Below:** Russian cartoon showing the German Imperialists' aspirations to control the whole of Europe, including the new Soviet State, after the 1914–18 war

Above: Soldiers and civilians digging graves near the Winter Palace for those killed in the street fighting. Below: Students and soldiers firing at the police in Petrograd

Grand Duke Dmitry's palace, the Oldenburg Palace and the Grand Duchess Olga's palace. Madame Narichkyna, chief lady-in-waiting at the Tsar's court, was now living in a small apartment and trying to raise money by negotiating with the *Louvre* in Paris to buy a valuable bust of *Marie Antoinette*, given by that lady herself to Madame Narichkyna's grandfather. There was something ironic in such a sale, thought Madame Lafarge – France would buy, at an enormous price, the head it had discarded just over a century ago!

She wondered what would happen now. It was strange, she reflected as she walked home, that most people who lived through historic times, as she was now doing, were, like herself, not impressed by or did not understand the great events taking place before their eyes. It was only afterwards that they realized, looking back, how vast and influential these events had been.

A car packed with soldiers came rapidly down the street, swerving round the unrepaired pot-holes. There were two men on the roof, four more on the running-boards. Soldiers lay at full length along the mudguards, their rifles pointing ahead; bayonets bristled from the windows. It was very dramatic, but frightening, for there, Madame Lafarge thought, was the Russia of the future.

All morning rumours had been growing in the barracks, and now Major Sokolov was in search of facts. He was heading for what he thought, mistakenly as it turned out, was the centre of power – the newly-formed *Council of the Russian Republic*. It was a body dominated by landlords and businessmen; the Bolsheviks had withdrawn almost immediately after it was established, and had called for a meeting of the *All-Russian Congress of Soviets*; meanwhile, they continued to control the now very powerful Petrograd Soviet.

The Council of the Russian Republic was meeting in the *Marrinsky Palace*. When Sokolov reached it, he found soldiers and an armoured car outside; there were barricades made of old wagons and timber, bits of looted furniture. At the main door of the palace a sailor was saying, "We just walked in there and filled all the doors with comrades. I went right up to the counter-revolutionary, Kornilovitz, who was in the president's chair. 'No more Council,' I said. 'Run along home now!' "

In fact, the Petrograd Military Revolutionary Committee, controlled by the Bolsheviks, had ordered the Council to dissolve itself. After a formal protest, the members walked away: "No more Council". In their short life since November 2, this body of landowners, professors, journalists, scientists, and intellectuals had been pitifully ineffective, arguing their time away in strictly parliamentary debates. Meanwhile, outside, the Petrograd Soviet, its messengers scurrying everywhere, prepared for the great day – November 7. And now the day was come.

Sokolov realized he had been wrong. The centre was not here; it was on the edge of the city at the *Smolny Institute* where the Petrograd Soviet was installed. This much was emphasized to him by the soldiers and Red Guards outside the Marrinsky Palace. Things had been moving fast, they said. The Bolsheviks had, as he well knew, the support of most of the Petrograd Garrison and they had armed detachments of Red Guards in every big factory. During the night, units had taken over the tele-

Above: Modern woodcut showing the Smolny Institute at night. **Below:** Photograph of the Smolny Institute as it appears today. Notice the statue of Lenin at the top of the avenue

Above: View from the Neva of the Winter Palace, built 1754–64. **Below:** The Russian battleship "Aurora"

phone exchange, the telegraph agency, the Baltic Station, the State Bank, the bridges over the Neva. It had all gone very smoothly, they told him complacently.

They had got in first, thought Sokolov. He had been told of plans made by Kerensky's Government on November 5 to arrest the Military Revolutionary Committee, suppress the Bolshevik newspapers, cut Smolny out of the telephone system and paralyse the plans for an *insurrection*. Kerensky's plans were not particularly secret; hearing of them, Lenin and *Trotsky*, the Bolshevik leaders, had said sarcastically that these were formidable orders "but it was not indicated who was to carry them out." That, of course, was Kerensky's weakness; his forces had gone over to the other side and all he had left was a newly-formed Women's Battalion and regiments of young cadets from the military training schools.

The *Winter Palace*, the soldiers said, was still holding out, even though there was a battleship, the *Aurora*, anchored in the Neva, its guns trained on the building. Sokolov turned towards the palace. . . .

Tamara Ivanova, unlike Major Sokolov, already knew which was the most important place in Petrograd that day. She was a delegate to the Petrograd Soviet at the Smolny Institute, and it was to this big yellow-painted building, that she was making her way by tramcar.

She had left the factory council in heated argument with Nikolai Saratov. "The Government says you're not to meet in working hours – this meeting is illegal," Saratov shouted. "Well, you try to stop us," the council retorted.

"Look," said Saratov persuasively, "I like a peaceful life, I'm a reasonable man. I'll pay you for all the time you spend talking, but really, friends, I can't give you another wage increase." "Nothing doing," said the council, "we've got to have that increase – look at the new food prices."

"OK, then I'll close the factory," snapped Saratov. So the argument went on. In the yard outside, the factory's Red Guard detachment was forming up. . . .

The Smolny Institute was roaring with activity. Lines of soldiers guarded the building, and at the main entrance were two quick-firing guns. In the courtyard stood dozens of cars and motor cycles, their engines running. A stream of couriers came and went, not only to factories and army barracks in Petrograd, but as far as Moscow, and strategic points even further away. In the hundred tall, white-painted rooms, where once the young ladies assembled for their classes in deportment and the social graces, there were now committees of dirty, tired, sleepless men and women – committees for supplies, for arms, for transport, for intelligence, for liaison with local soviets, for food distribution. The long corridors resounded with the tread of heavy boots.

Upstairs, the Military Revolutionary Committee, humming like a great dynamo, was issuing streams of orders, firing off proclamations.

Tamara, having had her credentials examined by four lots of sentries, decided to get some food before the vitally important meeting of the All-Russian Congress of Soviets opened its session. At a long table in the refectory she found a score of men and women handing out cabbage soup, hunks of black bread and tin cups full of tea. Other

A group of delegates at the first All-Russia Congress of Soviets in Petrograd in June 1917

A woman of South Russia dressed in traditional costume

A view of the Peter-Paul fortress in Petrograd

delegates had the same idea – bearded, long-haired peasants, workmen in black blouses, sailors from the *Kronstadt* naval base, and women in colourful national costume.

The session was to be held in the ballroom on the second floor, a great white salon with elaborate chandeliers. Behind the platform at one end was a blank gold picture frame – the portrait of the Tsar had been cut out. Here, duchesses and princes, generals and millionaires had danced only a few months previously.

Outside the Smolny Institute, close to one of the big bonfires the guards had made for themselves, sat Boris Melnikov. He had acquired from somewhere a shoeblack's outfit, and he was here because some of the street children had told him it was the busiest place in the city.

However, it seemed that all these people rushing in and out had no time at all for a shoeshine. So Boris sat there exchanging jokes and insults with the soldiers. One of them had given him some bread, which was very welcome, and he thought there might be a chance of some more if he stayed.

He heard the soldiers saying that the garrison of the *Peter-Paul fortress*, across the Neva river, had just come over to the side of the Soviet. They had been doubting and neutral until Trotsky made a speech to them; then they decided. So now the Soviet controlled the great *arsenal* in the fortress as well as the armament factories of Petrograd. Also, the Peter-Paul fortress could bombard the Winter Palace at any time.

A car drew up and a squat little man, wearing a round fur hat and a short overcoat, jumped out and hurried across the courtyard. He had a wide, rather humorous mouth and slanting, twinkling little eyes. He carried a brief-case, and as he looked a little tidier than some of the other men who went into the Smolny, Boris thought that here might be a customer. "Shoeshine, cheap—special price to you," he cried, barring the way. But the little man grinned, dodged round him and hurried on.

The sentries laughed. "*Tovarish* Lenin," they shouted to Boris, "has no time now. Maybe he'll make you *commissar* for State shoeshining after the revolution!"

Left: Soldiers and civilians reading news-sheets issued by the Duma. **Below:** Army officers standing by the Tsar's portrait in the Hall of the Duma, before the painting was removed

EVENING

Nikolai Saratov had left the factory council meeting with his mind made up. It was no use talking to these people; they would never see reason. It was time for something stronger than talk, and he knew where to go.

So here he was in the *Alexander Hall*, the *City Duma* building, which was still hung with Imperial portraits, now shrouded, though, in red cloth. He was listening with approval while Skobelev, chairman of a meeting of about a hundred people, urged that all anti-Bolshevik groups be united in one big organization, to be called the Committee for Salvation of Country and Revolution. There was general agreement. So Saratov saw the formation of the Committee for Salvation, the most determined and powerful opponent of the Bolsheviks. Members of the dissolved Council of the Republic were there, and so were leaders of the *Mensheviks* who had supported the Kerensky governments, and the *Socialist Revolutionaries*, who had parted company with the Bolsheviks months ago, to say nothing of members of the executive committee of the Petrograd Soviet, who had tried to sway the Soviet against the insurrection.

A few hours later, Saratov took part in another meeting of the Committee for Salvation. They were getting more and more support. The Union of Railway Workers had joined them, and the Post and Telegraph employees. The civil servants in the banks and ministries were taking part in passive resistance, refusing to support Bolshevik decrees. Postmen would not deliver or accept mail at Smolny, the telegraph men would not send messages, the railwaymen had cut off the city. And *Kaledin*, the Cossack leader, was marching north with an army.

It was not like the Soviet meeting. The people here were mainly businessmen, journalists, students, intellectuals of all camps, former specialist ministers. They assigned delegates to form committees in other cities; a committee to meet Kerensky; groups to visit banks, ministries and barracks – "Russian soldiers, do not shed the blood of your brothers!" Saratov was drawn willingly into all this activity. Here was something to do!

Above: Portrait engraving of a Cossack. **Below:** Chaos on the railways. An example of the result of passive resistance to the Bolshevik policy at the time

The streets were crowded again as Major Sokolov made his way towards the Winter Palace, where the ministers of the Provisional Government were still conferring. Alexander Kerensky was not there; he had gone to the battle front hoping to raise support among the troops. All the cars he might have used had been immobilized by the Bolsheviks, and he had travelled in a car borrowed from the American Embassy, flying the American flag. His exit from the scene was a little undignified; he found no troops to help him, returned in disguise to Petrograd, and, when the Bolsheviks issued a warrant for his arrest, he fled to England to become an exile for the rest of his life there and in America.

Tramcars were running, people were shopping and the theatres were open. In fact, Madame Lafarge went to hear a concern by *Chaliapin*, the world-famous singer, and came home safely by tram, though there was rifle-fire only a hundred yards away.

As Major Sokolov drew nearer the Winter Palace, the crowds thinned out and the streets became deserted. Suddenly he saw a mass of people, and – blocking their way – armed sailors drawn across the Nevsky Prospect. The crowd numbered several hundred – men in frock-coats, well-dressed women, army officers and many right-wing Socialist delegates who had walked out of the Congress of Soviets protesting against the tactics of the Bolsheviks. Now they wanted to see the Provisional Government.

White-bearded *Nikolai Schreider*, Mayor of Petrograd, and *S. N. Prokopovitch*, Minister of Supplies in the Provisional Government, were arguing with the sailors. "We insist; we must pass," said Schreider. Behind him there were shouts of "Shoot us if you like – have you the heart to fire on Russians and comrades?"

But the sailors were stubborn. They would not shoot, but neither would they let this crowd pass. Major Sokolov joined a fellow officer in the crowd and added his voice to the shouting. Then Prokopovitch, standing on a box, made a speech.

"Comrades and citizens," said Prokopovitch, waving his

The Nevsky Prospect, the main street in Petrograd, as it appears today

Lenin addressing the crowds in Red Square, Moscow, on November 7, 1918, on the first anniversary of the Revolution

umbrella, "Force is being used against us. We cannot have our innocent blood on the hands of these ignorant men. It is beneath our dignity to be shot down here in the street. Let us return to the Duma and discuss the best means of saving the country and the Revolution."

Whereupon, in dignified silence, the procession turned round and marched back up the Nevsky in columns of four. Major Sokolov went with them.

The great hall of the Smolny was now jammed with delegates to the All-Russian Soviet. People were sitting in the aisles, perched on the window ledges and on the edge of the platform. A blue cloud of cigarette smoke hung in the air; the atmosphere was foul. Tamara Ivanova hoped she would manage to sit through the session.

The session began at 10.40 in the evening with protests from the Socialist Revolutionaries that some of their members were besieged in the Winter Palace.

Then suddenly came one of the most dramatic moments of the whole revolution. A dull, heavy thud that brought delegates to their feet; then another and another. It was the boom of the cruiser "Aurora's" guns firing over the Winter Palace. Outside in the dark the last act of that crowded day was being decided by arms, and the knowledge of this brought a new urgency to the Congress.

The Mensheviks read a declaration: "Because the Bolsheviks have made a military conspiracy with the aid of the Petrograd Soviet without consulting the other factions and parties, we find it impossible to remain in the Congress, and therefore withdraw, inviting the other groups to follow us and to meet for discussion of the situation."

Immediate uproar and shouts of "Traitors" followed, in which Tamara joined. Then a delegate from another group declared dramatically that they would "perish with the Provisional Government in the Winter Palace – we will expose our breasts to the machine-guns of the terrorists." Fifty Menshevik delegates and their supporters pushed their way out amid jeers and boos. It was this group that took part in the brief encounter with sailors outside the Winter Palace.

The Hall of the Duma in Petrograd, where delegates from a number of regiments are attending a meeting, May 1917. The portrait of Tsar Nicholas II, which can be seen in the photograph on page 35, had been removed

Trotsky shouted from the platform: "Let them go! They will be swept into the garbage heap of history." Another Bolshevik leader announced that the Military Revolutionary Committee had sent a delegation to offer negotiations to the occupants of the Winter Palace.

After that, a night of furious debate took place during which exhausted delegates slept in their seats.

At one point there was a shout from the platform: "Thirty agitators wanted immediately for the front – report to Room 17." Upstairs, the Military Revolutionary Committee worked furiously; in the corridors unwashed men slept on the floor, clutching rifles in their sleep, undisturbed by feet hurrying all around them.

The delegates burst into cheers as *Nikolai Krylenko*, a Bolshevik leader, staggering with fatigue, climbed on to the platform and began to read a telegram: "Greetings from the 12th-Army. The Soldiers' Committee is taking command of the Northern Front."

Finally, at nearly six o'clock in the morning, a declaration was agreed: "The Provisional Government is deposed. Based on the will of the great majority of workers, peasants and soldiers, the Congress of Soviets assumes power. The Soviet authority will at once propose an immediate democratic peace to all nations, an immediate truce on all fronts. It will ensure the free transfer of lands to the Land Committees, defend the soldiers' rights, enforce a complete democratization of the army, establish workers' control over production. . . ."

Tamara walked home with others, excited, triumphant, singing, as the grey dawn rose over a Russia that to her had suddenly become a land bright with hope.

Boris Melnikov, tired after a long and not very successful day, was sleeping on a pile of canvas in a lorry. He was awakened by the thud of bundles being thrown down beside him. He sat up quickly. Soldiers were climbing in. The lorry shot off through the streets while the soldiers cut open the parcels and hurled white clouds of leaflets to passers-by. This was now the approved revolutionaries' method of leaflet distribution – a careering lorry with a trail of proclamations.

Trotsky, Bolshevik leader second only to Lenin as organizer of the Bolshevik revolution

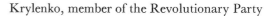

Krylenko, member of the Revolutionary Party

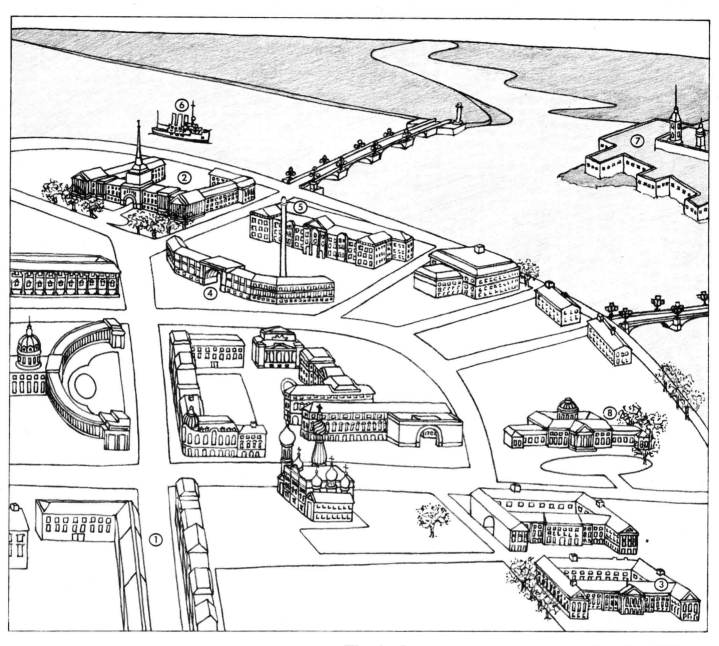

Plan of Central Petrograd showing all the important sites of activity of November 7, 1917: ① Nevsky Prospect ② The Admiralty ③ The Smolny Institute, Lenin's command post ④ Palace Square ⑤ The Winter Palace, headquarters of the Provisional Government ⑥ the battleship "Aurora" ⑦ the Peter-Paul fortress ⑧ the Tauride Palace

The leaflet was an announcement by the Military Revolutionary Committee: "State Power has passed into the hands of the organ of the Petrograd Soviet of Workers' and Soldiers' Deputies, the Military Revolutionary Committee, which stands at the head of the Petrograd *proletariat* and garrison. The cause for which the people were fighting: immediate proposal of a democratic peace, abolition of landlord property, adoption of rights over the land, labour control over production, creation of a Soviet Government – that cause is securely achieved."

Eventually the lorry was challenged and stopped by a cordon of soldiers at the entrance to the Palace Square. Boris jumped out into the street. There across the square were the long, lighted windows of the Winter Palace. At this point Boris forgot all about shoeshining and even about food. To him the Winter Palace had always been a dream, a fairy castle, something remote and frighteningly grand; and now there it was, so near.

Boris knew all about sentries and their ways. No line of guards in Russia could stop him if he wanted to slip past. He had little difficulty in finding an open door – most of them were open. Inside were long dark corridors and ancient attendants in brass-buttoned blue uniforms with red collars, who tried, not very seriously, to stop him. Upstairs, on the polished floors of rooms large and small, rows of dirty mattresses and blankets, cigarette ends, empty wine and champagne bottles looted from the cellars, were littered everywhere. Rifles were stacked on the floors, machine-guns mounted at windows.

Outside, there was a burst of rifle-fire. Inside, immediate frantic activity, soldiers shouting, "Here they come," grabbing rifles, rushing to the windows. But it was a false alarm; no attack this time. On the river, the guns of the "Aurora" and the Peter-Paul fortress began to boom. They were using only blank ammunition, as a warning, but they sounded terrible, and Boris ran back the way he had come.

Under the Red Arch, leading into the Palace Square, Red Guards and some soldiers were massed. Without any orders they moved forward; Boris followed them in the dark, his heart thudding with excitement. Over a barricade they climbed, over rifles thrown down by the defenders they ran – and there before them were open doors, light streaming out. This was the cellar of one wing in the palace. It was deserted and silent. Everywhere there were packing-cases, which the Red Guards battered open, pulling out an immense treasury of porcelain, pictures, statuettes, carpets, curtains and tapestries.

Boris wanted to see more. He followed groups running

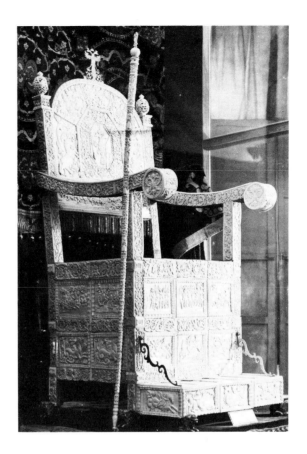

The ivory throne of Ivan the Terrible. One of the treasures of the Russian court, as is the egg (below), made of heliotrope enclosing a model of a battleship. This was made in Russia at the end of the 19th century

up the stairs. In one room the ministers of the Provisional Government sat round a table covered with green baize. They looked up as the Red Guards burst in and the leader shouted: "I am a member of the Military Revolutionary Committee. You are under arrest."

There followed arguments, interrogations, roll-calls, lists of names, before the protesting ministers were marched away, surrounded by guards with fixed bayonets.

In another part of the building, the defenders had surrendered; the Women's Battalion was locked in a large room; the military cadets were taken away. This final dissolution of the Provisional Government was almost bloodless. Five sailors and one soldier were killed, and a few others slightly wounded. A live shell from the "Aurora" knocked a chunk of plaster off the cornice of the palace and the façade was chipped by hundreds of rifle and machine-gun bullets. But not one of the defenders was hit.

Some looting took place, but it was checked; sheepish Red Guard soldiers were forced to disgorge what they had taken, by a self-appointed committee armed with revolvers. "The property of the people," they cried as they went through pockets and looked under coats. The defenders, too, had their loot, and the shouts of the committee were even louder as they were searched.

Through a silent crowd outside marched the ministers and their guards, on the way to the cells of the Peter-Paul fortress. Beyond the Palace Square there were angry shouts and demands for lynching as the little procession passed; on the bridge over the Neva a burst of rifle-fire sent ministers and guards diving to the ground. Later, the ministers were to be released; they were, after all, not very competent in their opposition, just a rather bewildered group of men who had pursued a policy they thought right amid forces they could never control. The real fight was to be with the Committee for Salvation, now preparing for *civil war*.

Boris knew nothing of all this, nor would he have been interested. He had to think of tomorrow's food, tomorrow's problems of survival. Looking at the ministers' good boots as they straggled along, he thought sadly that there might have been a lot of good business there.

An example of the luxurious furnishings in the Alexander Palace at Tsarkoe Selo, near Petrograd. It was the home of the Tsar Nicholas II and his family, and this is the Tsarina's room

Glossary

Alexander III (1845–1894)   Tsar of Russia, son of Alexander II. During his reign he formed strong allegiances with France

Alexander Hall   government administration offices in St. Petersburg

Alexandrinsky Theatre   building in Petrograd used for the Democratic Conference in September 1917, initiated by Kerensky

All-Russian Congress of Soviets   the first meeting of this body was organized by the Bolsheviks and held on June 16, 1917

arsenal   an establishment for making and storing weapons

Aurora   a Russian cruiser which, although ordered away on a training cruise, since it was thought dangerously near the Winter Palace, was brought back by the crew who were sympathetic to the insurrection. It played a significant role in the capture of the Palace

autocrat   absolute ruler. One who assumes total responsibility for decision-making

Balaclava   a point near the Black Sea in S. Crimea, USSR. It was the scene of the charge of the Light Brigade in 1854 during the Crimean War (between Russia and the allied powers of Turkey, England, France and Sardinia, 1853–56). A Balaclava helmet is a woollen covering for the head and shoulders, worn especially by soldiers on active service

Bolsheviks   these were members of the revolutionary Marxist party who believed that the workers should unite with the poverty-stricken peasants in the struggle against the bourgeois society, to work towards a socialist state

bureaucrats   those involved in centralized government

Catherine the Great (1729–1796)   Empress Catherine II of Russia, daughter of a German prince, wife of Peter III of Russia. Despite plans for reform, she was hampered by the landowning classes and her reign was marked by imperialist expansion and an extension of serfdom

Chaliapin, Fedor Ivanovich (1873–1938)   Russian bass opera singer noted for his dramatic prowess

City Duma   The St. Petersburg Municipal Council

civil war   this sprang up very shortly after the Revolution. It was an armed resistance to the new Bolshevik government, caused by widespread peasant discontent, and protest against the Bolshevik dictatorship in Moscow. Trotsky was a driving force in organizing the Red Guard into the Red Army. Peace was restored by 1920 and Lenin remained in control during and after the war, until his death in 1924. The war was much prolonged by the intervention of troops from Britain, Japan, America, France and other countries, against the Bolsheviks

commissar   at that time, the name of the head of a government department or group in the armed forces

Comrades   an emotional term of address used to evoke the revolutionaries' ideal of all men fighting for the cause of equality and brotherhood

Cossacks   community of peasants and landowners with land in the Caucasus, Siberia, near the Volga, and other areas. They were richer than most other peasants and were given special privileges, such as exemption from taxes and allocations of land, in return for military service under the Tsars

Council of the Russian Republic   successor to the Democratic conference. Also called the Preparliament. It was formed, its first session being in October 1917, as an interim, all-representative body, that would fill the gap until the Constituent Assembly, the long-established dream of the Russian democrats. It had 550

	members, including the cream of the intelligentsia, although it was "officially powerless"
Countess Kleinmichel	was later (i.e. after the time of this book) arrested and, while under arrest, is reported to have observed that officers held by the revolutionaries "looked like sheep led to the slaughter"
Deputies	these were the elected local representatives of the groups of workers and soldiers
Duma	the Russian parliament, limited in power and based on a greatly restricted voting population. It was set up as a result of the 1905 revolution
Grand Duke Dmitry	a favourite of the Tsar. An accomplice in the murder of Gregory Rasputin, in December 1916
Grand Duke Michael	brother of Nicholas whose nomination for accession to the throne of Russia in March 1917 was rejected outright
insurrection	a rising against the established authority. The word implies a specific action which is aimed at taking over state power
Kaledin, Alexi	General in charge of the Cossacks – committed suicide during the civil war when denounced by his men in favour of the Bolsheviks
Kerensky, Alexander Fyodorovich	this man was leader of the Trudoviks (a group of intellectuals who defended the peasants against the landowners, but did not tend very far to the left) in the fourth Duma. After the October revolution, he emigrated to New York, USA
khaki	a dull yellow dusty colour. The word was adopted to describe a twill material, particularly used for army uniforms
knout	this was a type of whip, often fatal in its effects
kopeks	Russian copper coins. One kopek was the hundredth part of a rouble
Kornilov, General Lavr Georgevich (1870–1918)	he succeeded Khabalov in command of the military district of Petrograd. He subsequently tried to establish a military dictatorship but was defeated by the Bolsheviks
Kronstadt	an island fortress and naval base in the Gulf of Finland, guarding St. Petersburg; it was founded by Peter the Great in 1710. The men hated many of their officers and murdered them. Thus, this base was the scene of the major naval mutiny which helped to precipitate the Revolution
krushka	a jug
Krylenko, Nikolai	a prominent Bolshevik agitator at the front
Kuznetsk	a town in southern Siberia; now an important industrial area
Lenin, Vladimir Ilyich (1870–1924)	was the head of the Bolshevik party and leader of the Revolution. He became first head of the Soviet Government, a post which he held undisputed until his death
Little Hunch-backed Horse, The	Ballet. Music composed in 1864 by Arthur Michel Faint-Léon
Louvre	an ancient royal palace in Paris which is today (and was in 1917) one of the richest museums and art galleries in the world
mazagine	a store for arms and ammunition, gunpowder and other explosives
March	in March 1917 the Tsar abdicated. The Provisional Government was set up and the Moscow soviet had its first session
Marie Antoinette (1755–1793)	wife of Louis XVI; queen of France. Both she and her husband were accused of treason and were guillotined during the French Revolution
Marrinsky Palace	palace in Petrograd where the Ministry of the Provisional Government held its meetings
Marseillaise	a favourite revolutionary song, originally composed in France in 1792 after the French Revolution
Mensheviks	one wing of the Russian Social-Democratic workers' party after it split in 1903, the other being the Bolsheviks. In 1912 both parties were

established individually. Mensheviks were less rigid than the Bolsheviks about membership of the party. They believed in a revolution brought about by the whole working class rather than by a highly trained elite

Milyukov, Paul Nikolayevich (1859–1943) a professor of history, founder and head of the Kadet party. He was Minister of Foreign Affairs and at one stage ran the Provisional Government. After the October revolution he fought the Bolsheviks energetically but was later discouraged and emigrated to Paris

Moscow city on the Moskva River, south of Petrograd (now Leningrad). Ancient capital of Russia, superseded by St. Petersburg at the beginning of the 18th century. It became the capital for the second time in 1917 after the Bolshevik victory

Neva, River this is the river on which Leningrad (then Petrograd) stands. It flows out into the Gulf of Finland at Lagoda

Nevsky Prospect the main avenue of Leningrad

Nicholas II (1868–1918) last Emperor and Tsar of Russia, son of Alexander III. He and his family were shot in July 1918

Peter the Great Peter I (1672–1725), Emperor of Russia from the age of 10. Created St. Petersburg as the capital in 1703

Peter-Paul fortress a formidable prison fortress on an island in St. Petersburg

Petrograd the name given by the revolutionaries to St. Petersburg—the capital of Russia during the latter part of Tsarist rule. Now renamed Leningrad. Moscow became the new capital for the second time in 1917

Preobrazhensky regiment whose commissar was A. S. Chudnovsky

profiteers men who make huge profits because of the plight of a society, in times of food or equipment shortage

Prokopovitch, S. N. Minister of Supplies (Trade and Industry) in the Provisional Government. A writer who, according to Trotsky, professed allegiance to no particular party but was "dwelling on the borderland between Kadets and Mensheviks"

proletariat the working class

Provisional Government this was formed on March 15, 1917, by the Provisional Committee of the Duma, with the support of the Soviet, and with Kerensky as Minister of Justice

Putilov between July 3–5, 1917, the factory workers of Petrograd staged a violent strike. The overall purpose of this demonstration was to bring down the Provisional Government and replace it with one that more directly represented the wishes of the workers and soldiers

Queen Victoria (1819–1901) Queen of Great Britain from 1837 to the end of her life

Red Guards a workers' militia which, at its formation, was very popular and attracted queues of volunteers ready to join

Reed, John (1879–1925) American journalist who wrote the famous eye-witness account of the October uprisings in Petrograd, "Ten Days that Shook the World". Later he was one of the founders of the Communist party in the USA

regime a regime is any form of government. In this case it refers to the rule of the Tsars

Republic a state in which government is effected by the people or through its elected representatives

Riga is the capital of Latvia, USSR, situated on the Baltic Sea. Now a great industrial and dairy produce area

Rockefeller, John Davison (1839–1937) American millionaire who made a fortune out of oil, and lived a philanthropic life, donating large sums of money to good causes. The Rockefeller Foundation has continued this work since his death

Rodichev, F. I. a Kadet, favouring constitutional monarchy, and even ultimately a republic; a lawyer and landowner. He denounced the workers at one stage for

	having appropriated from France "the shameful slogan: get rich!"
Romanov	royal household of Russia for 300 years until the Revolution in 1917
rouble	Russian monetary unit and silver coin
sabres	cavalry sword with curved blades
Schreider, Nikolai	a Social Revolutionary; Mayor or burgomaster of Petrograd
second revolution	this refers to the successful uprising of the Bolsheviks, led by Lenin on November 7, 1917, which ended in the seizure of Petrograd
serfs	peasants who were bound to a member of the landowning class. The landowner could dispose of the person, the labour and the property of the peasants belonging to him as he chose. The serfs in Russia were finally emancipated by Tsar Alexander II in 1861
shells	large explosives for use in big guns or mortars
Skobelev, Matthew Ivanovich (1885–1939)	was a member of the fourth Duma; one of the leaders of the Menshevik party, he became Minister of Labour in the Coalition Government. At the time of the Revolution he was anti-Bolshevik
Smolny Institute	before the Revolution, this was a school for girls of the aristocracy and nobility. It was occupied by the Petrograd Soviet when it moved from the Tauride Palace
socialist	based on socialism, a political and economic theory of social organization, involving ownership by the State of products, means of production, distribution and exchange, thus promoting social and economic equality
Socialist Revolutionaries	formed at the beginning of the twentieth century as a peasant socialist party. Though stronger in numbers than the Bolsheviks, they were ineffective in their opposition to the

	October insurrection. Usually called SR's
soviets	this is the Russian word for "council". Here it refers to the councils of workers', soldiers' and later peasants' representatives
Tabel o Ravgov	a "Table of Ranks", drawn up by Peter the Great regarding the dress of his subjects. It even went so far as to abolish beards and the old costume of the people, so that everyone would display on his dress, on buttons and shoulder straps, the insignia of the Tsar
Tovarish	Russian for "Comrade"
Trotsky, Leon Davidovich (1879–1940)	a marxist who joined the Bolsheviks in May 1917. Second only to Lenin as organizer of the Bolshevik insurrection; also founder of the Red Army. He was dislodged from power by Stalin shortly after Lenin's death, when he was exiled to Siberia; in 1929 he was exiled from Russia altogether. He was assassinated in Mexico by a Stalinist in 1940. Great writer, speaker, philosopher and man of action.
Tsar	head of the monarchy in Russia during Imperial rule
Tsarina Alexandra	Tsarina was the term used for the wife of the Tsar. Alexandra Feodorovna (1872–1918) was a German princess, daughter of the Duke of Hesse. She was shot with her husband and family in 1918
Tsarism	rule by the Tsars
Tsarskoe Selo	a town near Petrograd, the location of one of the Tsar's palaces
valinki	high felt boots
war	this refers to World War I (1914–1918). Germany declared war on Russia on August 1, 1914
Winter Palace	the official residence of the Tsar in St. Petersburg

Index

Further Reading

A Short History of the Russian Revolution, Joel Carmichael (London: Nelson, 1966)

Russian Revolution, Anthony Cash (Garden City: Doubleday & Co. Inc., 1969)

Fall of the Winter Palace; November 1917, Robert Goldston (New York: Franklin Watts, Inc., 1971)

The Russian Revolution, Robert Goldston (London: J. M. Dent, 1967; New York: Bobbs-Merrill Co., Inc., 1966)

Lenin and the Russian Revolution, Christopher Hill (London: English Universities Press, 1967)

The Evolution of Russia, Otto Hoetzsch (London: Thames & Hudson, 1966)

The Growth of Modern Russia, John Kennett (Glasgow: Blackie, 1970)

Russian Revolution, Lionel Kochan (New York: The John Day Company, 1970)

Russian Revolution, Lionel Kochan (New York: G. P. Putnam's Sons, 1972)

Russia, John Lawrence (London: Methuen, 1965)

Ten Days that Shook the World, John Reed (Middlesex: Penguin, 1970)

Russia of the Tsars 1796–1917, David Smith (London: Ernest Benn, 1971)

The First Book of the Soviet Union, Louis L. Snyder (New York: Franklin Watts, Inc., 1972)

History of the Russian Revolution, Leon Trotsky *trans.* Max Eastman (London: Victor Gollancz Ltd., 1965)